## HAL•LEONARD

# JAZZ PLAY-ALONG®

Book & Audio for B♭, E♭, C and Bass Clef Instruments

# LATIN JAZZ
# STANDARDS
## 10 CLASSIC TUNES

**volume 96**

**Arranged and Produced by Mark Taylor**

**PLAYBACK+**
Speed • Pitch • Balance • Loop

To access audio, visit:
**www.halleonard.com/mylibrary**

5358-8282-1880-3356

ISBN 978-1-4234-5911-8

## HAL•LEONARD®

Visit Hal Leonard Online at
**www.halleonard.com**

World headquarters, contact:
**Hal Leonard**
7777 West Bluemound Road
Milwaukee, WI 53213
Email: info@halleonard.com

In Europe, contact:
**Hal Leonard Europe Limited**
1 Red Place
London, W1K 6PL
Email: info@halleonardeurope.com

In Australia, contact:
**Hal Leonard Australia Pty. Ltd.**
4 Lentara Court
Cheltenham, Victoria, 3192 Australia
Email: info@halleonard.com.au

HAL•LEONARD®

Visit Hal Leonard Online at **www.halleonard.com**

Explore the entire family of Hal Leonard products and resources

# Latin Jazz Standards

HAL•LEONARD

JAZZ PLAY-ALONG®

## Volume 96

## Arranged and Produced by
## Mark Taylor

### Featured Players:

Graham Breedlove–Trumpet
Scott Silbert–Tenor Saxophone
Tony Nalker–Piano
Jim Roberts–Bass
Joe McCarthy–Drums

**Recorded at Bias Studios, Springfield, Virginia**
**Bob Dawson, Engineer**

## HOW TO USE THE AUDIO:

Each song has two tracks:

### 1) Split Track/Demonstration

**Woodwind, Brass, Keyboard,** and **Mallet Players** can use this track as a learning tool for melody style and inflection.

**Bass Players** can learn and perform with this track – remove the recorded bass track by turning down the volume on the LEFT channel.

**Keyboard** and **Guitar Players** can learn and perform with this track – remove the recorded piano part by turning down the volume on the RIGHT channel.

### 2) Backing Track

**Soloists** or **Groups** can learn and perform with this accompaniment track with the RHYTHM SECTION only.

# ADIOS

ENGLISH WORDS BY EDDIE WOODS
SPANISH TRANSLATION AND MUSIC BY ENRIC MADRIGUERA

C VERSION

# BAIA
## (BAHÍA)

C VERSION

MUSIC AND PORTUGUESE LYRIC BY ARY BARROSO
ENGLISH LYRIC BY RAY GILBERT

# Bésame Mucho
## (KISS ME MUCH)

C VERSION

WORDS AND MUSIC BY
CONSUELO VELAZQUEZ

# BRAZIL

ORIGINAL WORDS AND MUSIC BY ARY BARROSO
ENGLISH LYRICS BY S.K. RUSSELL

C VERSION

# THE BREEZE AND I

WORDS BY AL STILLMAN
MUSIC BY ERNESTO LECUONA

C VERSION

# POINCIANA
## (SONG OF THE TREE)

WORDS BY BUDDY BERNIER
MUSIC BY NAT SIMON

VERSION

# QUIZÁS, QUIZÁS, QUIZÁS
## (PERHAPS, PERHAPS, PERHAPS)

C VERSION

MUSIC AND SPANISH WORDS BY OSVALDO FARRES
ENGLISH WORDS BY JOE DAVIS

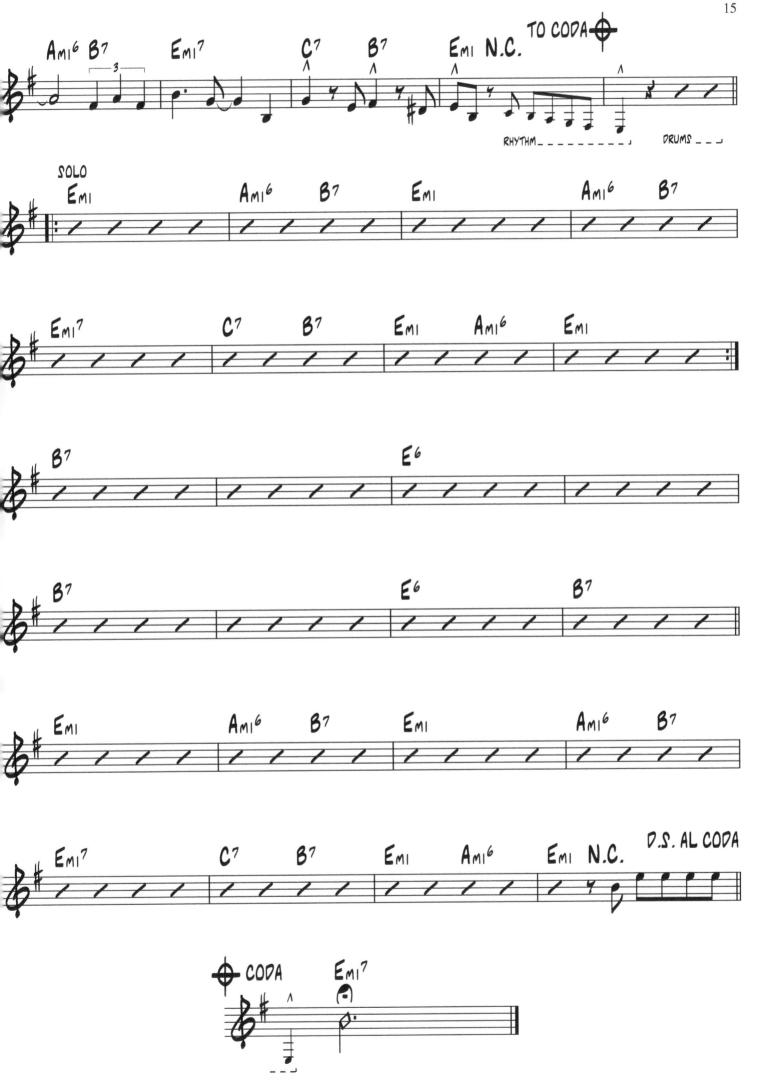

# TICO, TICO
## (TICO TICO NO FUBA)

MUSIC BY ZEQUINHA ABREU
ALOYSIO OLIVEIRA AND ERVIN DRAKE

C VERSION

MEDIUM SAMBA

# WHAT NOW MY LOVE

ORIGINAL FRENCH LYRIC BY PIERRE DELANO
MUSIC BY FRANCOIS BECAUD
ENGLISH ADAPTATION BY CARL SIGMAN

C VERSION

# YOU BELONG TO MY HEART
## (SOLAMENTE UNA VEZ)

MUSIC AND SPANISH WORDS BY
AGUSTÍN LARA

C VERSION

# You Belong to My Heart
## (Solamente Una Vez)

MUSIC AND SPANISH WORDS BY
AGUSTÍN LARA

# ADIOS

ENGLISH WORDS BY EDDIE WOODS
SPANISH TRANSLATION AND MUSIC BY ENRIC MADRIGUERA

Bb Version

23

# BAIA
## (BAHÍA)

Bb VERSION

MUSIC AND PORTUGUESE LYRIC BY ARY BARROSO
ENGLISH LYRIC BY RAY GILBERT

# Bésame Mucho
## (Kiss Me Much)

Bb Version

WORDS AND MUSIC BY
CONSUELO VELAZQUEZ

# BRAZIL

ORIGINAL WORDS AND MUSIC BY ARY BARROSO
ENGLISH LYRICS BY S.K. RUSSELL

Bb VERSION

# THE BREEZE AND I

WORDS BY AL STILLMAN
MUSIC BY ERNESTO LECUONA

# POINCIANA
## (SONG OF THE TREE)

WORDS BY BUDDY BERNIER
MUSIC BY NAT SIMON

# QUIZÁS, QUIZÁS, QUIZÁS
## (PERHAPS, PERHAPS, PERHAPS)

Bb VERSION

MUSIC AND SPANISH WORDS BY OSVALDO FARRES
ENGLISH WORDS BY JOE DAVIS

# TICO, TICO
## (TICO TICO NO FUBA)

MUSIC BY ZEQUINHA ABREU
ALOYSIO OLIVEIRA AND ERVIN DRAKE

Bb VERSION

# WHAT NOW MY LOVE

ORIGINAL FRENCH LYRIC BY PIERRE DELANOE
MUSIC BY FRANCOIS BECAUD
ENGLISH ADAPTATION BY CARL SIGMAN

Bb VERSION

# ADIOS

ENGLISH WORDS BY EDDIE WOODS
SPANISH TRANSLATION AND MUSIC BY ENRIC MADRIGUERA

Eb VERSION

# BAIA
## (BAHÍA)

Eb Version

MUSIC AND PORTUGUESE LYRIC BY ARY BARROSO
ENGLISH LYRIC BY RAY GILBERT

# Bésame Mucho
## (Kiss Me Much)

Eb Version

WORDS AND MUSIC BY
CONSUELO VELAZQUEZ

# BRAZIL

ORIGINAL WORDS AND MUSIC BY ARY BARROSO
ENGLISH LYRICS BY S.K. RUSSELL

# THE BREEZE AND I

WORDS BY AL STILLMAN
MUSIC BY ERNESTO LECUONA

Eb VERSION

# POINCIANA
## (SONG OF THE TREE)

WORDS BY BUDDY BERNIER
MUSIC BY NAT SIMON

# QUIZÁS, QUIZÁS, QUIZÁS
## (PERHAPS, PERHAPS, PERHAPS)

Eb VERSION

MUSIC AND SPANISH WORDS BY OSVALDO FARRES
ENGLISH WORDS BY JOE DAVIS

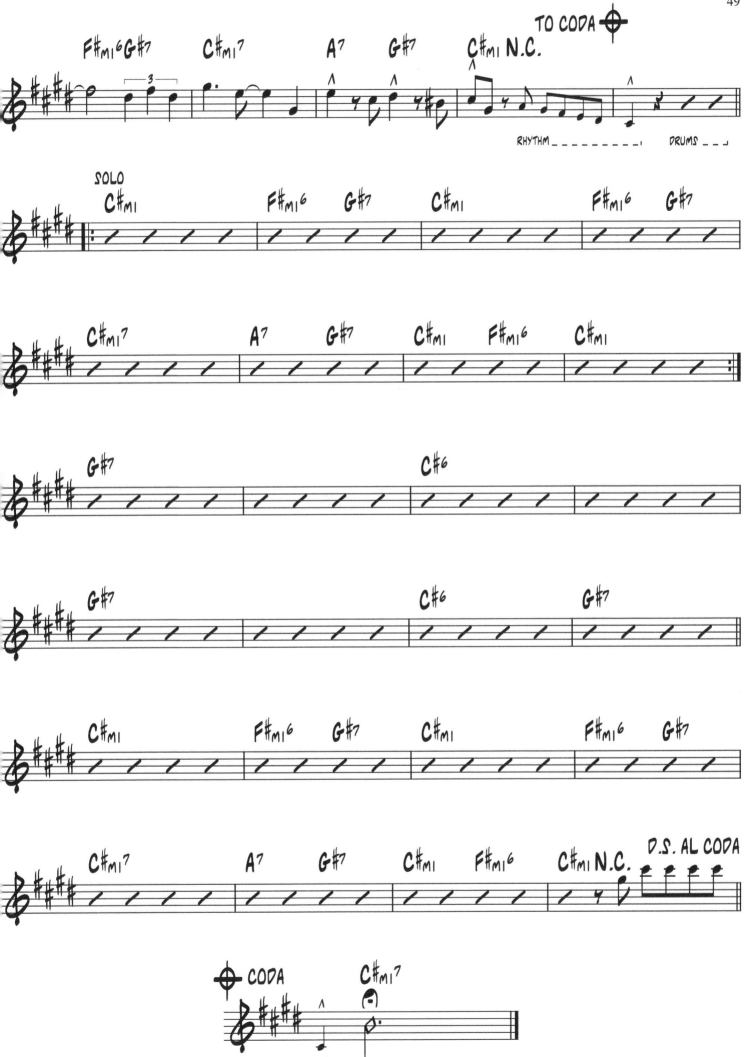

# TICO, TICO
## (TICO TICO NO FUBA)

MUSIC BY ZEQUINHA ABREU,
ALOYSIO OLIVEIRA AND ERVIN DRAKE

Eb VERSION

# WHAT NOW MY LOVE

ORIGINAL FRENCH LYRIC BY PIERRE DELANO
MUSIC BY FRANCOIS BECAUD
ENGLISH ADAPTATION BY CARL SIGMAN

Eb VERSION

53

# You Belong to My Heart
### (Solamente Una Vez)

MUSIC AND SPANISH WORDS BY
AGUSTÍN LARA

# You Belong to My Heart
## (Solamente Una Vez)

MUSIC AND SPANISH WORDS BY
AGUSTÍN LARA

# ADIOS

ENGLISH WORDS BY EDDIE WOODS
SPANISH TRANSLATION AND MUSIC BY ENRIC MADRIGUERA

# BAIA
## (BAHÍA)

MUSIC AND PORTUGUESE LYRIC BY ARY BARROSO
ENGLISH LYRIC BY RAY GILBERT

# Bésame Mucho
## (KISS ME MUCH)

WORDS AND MUSIC BY
CONSUELO VELAZQUEZ

𝄢: C VERSION

# BRAZIL

ORIGINAL WORDS AND MUSIC BY ARY BARROSO
ENGLISH LYRICS BY S.K. RUSSELL

# THE BREEZE AND I

WORDS BY AL STILLMAN
MUSIC BY ERNESTO LECUONA

# POINCIANA
## (SONG OF THE TREE)

WORDS BY BUDDY BERNIER
MUSIC BY NAT SIMON

C VERSION

# QUIZÁS, QUIZÁS, QUIZÁS
## (PERHAPS, PERHAPS, PERHAPS)

9: C VERSION

MUSIC AND SPANISH WORDS BY OSVALDO FARRES
ENGLISH WORDS BY JOE DAVIS

# TICO, TICO
## (TICO TICO NO FUBA)

MUSIC BY ZEQUINHA ABREU,
ALOYSIO OLIVEIRA AND ERVIN DRAKE

# WHAT NOW MY LOVE

ORIGINAL FRENCH LYRIC BY PIERRE DELANO
MUSIC BY FRANCOIS BECAUD
ENGLISH ADAPTATION BY CARL SIGMAN

C VERSION

71